MARKUS "NOTCH" PERSSON

BETA 87C

MARKUS "NOTCH" PERSSON

MINECRAFT MOGUL

MATT DOEDEN

LERNER PUBLICATIONS ◆ MINNEAPOLIS

Lerner Publications Company
A division of Lerner Publishing Group, Inc.
241 First Avenue North
Minneapolis, MN USA 55401

For reading levels and more information, look up this title at www.lernerbooks.com.

Image credits: Robert Kluba/REA/Redux, pp. 2, 6, 32, 34; Max Photography for GDC Online/Flickr (CC BY 2.0), p. 8; Surie/Shutterstock.com, p. 9; Daniel Hägglund/Flickr (CC BY-NC-SA 2.0), p. 10; 3d_kot/Shutterstock.com, p. 11; The Advertising Archives/Alamy Stock Photo, p. 12; Wurm Online, p. 14; Rick Friedman/Corbis/Getty Images, p. 15; Blast Passage via YouTube, p. 17; Chesnot/Getty Images, p. 19; Shadowman39/Flidkr (CC BY 2.0), p. 21; David McNew/Getty Images, p. 21; Minecraft screengrab, pp. 23, 24, 25; Peter Skaugvold/ZUMA Press/Newscom, p. 26; Ints Kalnins/Reuters/Newscom, pp. 27, 36; Zuma Press/Newscom, p. 29; Yui Mok/PA Images/Getty Images, p. 30; Andrew Chin/Getty Images, p. 33; Gabe Ginsberg/FilmMagic/Getty Images, p. 37; CelebrityHomePhotos/Newscom, p. 39; Official GDC/Trish Tunney/Flickr (CC BY 2.0), p. 40; picmov/Getty Images, p. 41.

Cover: Yui Mok/PA Images/Getty Images (Markus Persson); Christoph Sauer/Pixabay CC0 (landscape).

Main body text set in Rotis Serif Std 55 Regular 13.5/17. Typeface provided by Adobe Systems.

Library of Congress Cataloging-in-Publication Data

Names: Doeden, Matt, author.
Title: Markus Notch Persson, Minecraft mogul / Matt Doeden.
Description: Minneapolis : Lerner Publications, [2019] | Series: Gateway biographies | Includes bibliographical references and index.
Identifiers: LCCN 2018005349 (print) | LCCN 2018002341 (ebook) | ISBN 9781541524507 (eb pdf) | ISBN 9781541524460 (lb : alk. paper)
Subjects: LCSH: Persson, Markus, 1979–Juvenile literature. | Computer programmers–Sweden–Biography–Juvenile literature. | Minecraft (Game)–Juvenile literature. | Computer games–Design–Juvenile literature.
Classification: LCC GV1469.35.M535 (print) | LCC GV1469.35.M535 D64 2019 (ebook) | DDC 794.8092 [B]–dc23

LC record available at https://lccn.loc.gov/2018005349

Manufactured in the United States of America
1-44526-34776-5/9/2018

CONTENTS

Markus "Notch" Persson is known worldwide for *Minecraft*, the video game he created.

On November 18, 2011, the Mandalay Bay Hotel in Las Vegas, Nevada, was crawling with brightly colored boxes. People swarmed the hotel's casino with boxes on their heads. They wore boxes on their bodies. All the people and their boxes were there for one reason: MineCon. It was a celebration of *Minecraft*, a video game that had taken the gaming world by storm. Fans were also eager to lay eyes on the game's creator, Markus "Notch" Persson.

The crowd of about five thousand people, many wearing box costumes designed to look like *Minecraft* characters, converged on the hotel's convention center. There, Persson, dressed in jeans, a black shirt, and his trademark black fedora, waited near the main stage. The crowd cheered and clapped as, one by one, the people who had helped create *Minecraft* were introduced.

Lydia Winters, the brand director for the game, addressed the crowd. "This all started because of one person," she began. The crowd roared.

In 2011 Lydia Winters started working for the company that owns *Minecraft*. Her first job title there was "director of fun."

"I think we need to do better than that!" Winters continued. "I think we need to chant to get him up on stage."

The chant rose up. "Notch! Notch! Notch!" The people were calling Persson's screen name—the name he uses in *Minecraft*.

Persson climbed onto the stage. In the months leading up to MineCon, he'd become something of a celebrity. But he was not used to this kind of attention. Winters tried to get Persson to speak, but he appeared nervous and said little.

The highlight of MineCon had arrived. It was the moment when *Minecraft 1.0* would finally get its official release. Until then the game had existed only as an unfinished product. Gamers could download early versions, which they'd heard about primarily through word of mouth. Those limits hadn't stopped its tremendous popularity, though.

Persson stepped up to a large lever. He pushed it, setting off fireworks and a shower of confetti. The crowd went wild as loud music pumped through the convention center. It was official: *Minecraft 1.0* was live and available to purchase.

Persson looked out over the crowd of gaming fans as someone announced that four thousand people were already logging into *Minecraft 1.0* every second. A gaming revolution had begun, and Persson was at the center of it.

From the outside, it looked as though all of Persson's dreams were coming true. But while no one could have known it at the time, the game developer was beginning to feel trapped by the game he'd created. *Minecraft* had taken a huge role in Persson's life in recent years, putting him under pressure from fans and leaving him with little time to create new projects. Even as he watched the celebration at MineCon, he was looking for a way to escape.

People play *Minecraft* on smartphones, tablets, laptops, and desktop computers.

BUILDING BLOCKS

Markus Alexej Persson was born June 1, 1979, in Stockholm, Sweden. When he was a baby, he moved with his parents to the small town of Edsbyn. His mother, Ritva Persson, was a nurse. His father, Birger Persson, worked for a railroad company.

As a child in Edsbyn, Markus loved playing with the other kids in his neighborhood. He was a social kid with lots of friends. But all of that changed when he was seven. That's when the family, which included his little sister, Anna, moved to Stockholm. Markus struggled to make friends in his new school. He spent much of his time at home, playing with Lego blocks. He lost himself in the toys, creating spaceships, cars, and anything else he could imagine. Lego held his attention in a way that other toys didn't. Building his own creations appealed to him. Lego opened a world limited only by his imagination.

Building with Lego consumed Markus's free time—until his father brought home something

Edsbyn, the town where Markus spent his early childhood

Markus's favorite early-childhood activity was building with Lego blocks.

new. It was a home computer, called a Commodore 128. Markus was fascinated with the machine. The computer's cartridge-based games were fun. But they weren't what really captivated the seven-year-old. The computer also came with an instruction book on how to write computer programs. For Markus, the idea that he could create his own games from the ground up was irresistible. With the book as his guide, he began entering lines of computer code into the machine. He became so obsessed that he sometimes pretended to be sick so that he could stay home from school and work on the computer.

"We started subscribing to a computer magazine," Markus later said. "It had program listings in it that you could enter into your computer to get a silly little game or fun effect and things like that. I started entering them, and noticed that they broke or did different things if you changed what you entered. I don't remember exactly how fast this process was, but I know I made my first own program when I was eight years old."

A 1980s advertisement for the Commodore 128 computer

That first program was a simple text-based adventure game set in the Old West of the United States. It was really more of a story than a game. One would read text and then type in a choice to guide the story. It didn't include graphics or sound—just words and choices. Yet for a self-taught eight-year-old, it was an impressive feat. Still, Markus had a lot to learn. He didn't know how to save his games. So every time someone turned off the computer, he'd lose what he'd created.

When Markus was twelve, his parents divorced. His father moved out, and the rest of his family soon moved into a small apartment. He saw less and less of his dad, who struggled with a drug problem. His sister rebelled. She turned to drugs and violence and eventually left home. It was a difficult time. Markus found his escape through his computer. He grew more and more isolated, at home as well as at school.

"He preferred to just sit indoors," said his mother. "I tried everything to get him outside, signed him up for sports, football, everything, but it didn't work."

Markus's life was filled with change. But one thing stayed the same. Markus knew what he wanted to do with his life. He wanted to make computer games.

CHASING THE DREAM

Persson was unhappy at high school. After graduating, he continued to live at home with his mom, in no hurry to find a job and move out on his own. One day, his mother saw a newspaper listing for a course on computer programming. She was eager for her son to find his own way, so she signed him up without even asking him.

Meanwhile, Persson continued to work on his own games at home. He entered coding contests, and his skill and creativity began to shine through. Still, with little formal training, finding a job in the gaming industry was difficult. He worked at several programming jobs outside of the computer gaming field, but he didn't stick with any of them. Although Persson could do the work, he found most programming jobs dull.

Things started to turn around in 2002, when Persson was in his early twenties. He got a job with a company called Game Federation. The company focused not on making games but on distributing them. However, it needed coders to create prototypes, or sample programs, for various gaming systems. It wasn't quite Persson's dream job, but it at least put him in the right field.

At Game Federation, Persson met fellow programmer Rolf Jansson. The two quickly struck up a friendship. They mostly played video games together, often talking about what they thought was missing in the gaming industry. Then they focused on building a massively multiplayer online (MMO) game. These sorts of games, played on the internet, featured vast worlds and players from around the globe. In their free time, the pair dreamed up an MMO game called *Wurm Online*. By 2003 a beta—or testable—version was ready for release. *Wurm* allowed players to gather in a virtual space to build

In *Wurm Online*, players in different places can work together to survive in surroundings they create themselves.

The MMO game *EverQuest*, launched in 1999, influenced many MMO games that came after it.

a community or wage war. Players built cities, dug mines, gathered resources, and fought enemies, all on a shared server. The idea of an MMO game was not new. But few had gained enough popularity to build large communities.

Meanwhile, Persson continued to search for a job more in line with his career goals. In 2004 Persson took a job with a small, up-and-coming game developer called Midasplayer. The company focused on web-based games. At first, it felt like a perfect fit for Persson. He was finally doing what he'd always wanted to do. The games he helped to create were small in scope compared with the ones he imagined creating. But aside from that, it was his dream job. And he was earning enough money to move out of his mother's house and get an apartment of his own.

As the months passed, though, Persson grew frustrated with his job. Midasplayer judged its games almost entirely by how many people played them. That meant that the company often created the same sorts of games. They made sequels and then sequels to the sequels. Persson was making games, but he didn't really get to use his creativity. What had seemed like a dream job had become . . . just a job.

SEARCHING FOR ESCAPE

Meanwhile, *Wurm Online* quickly grew in popularity. The game gave Persson the creative outlet he was lacking at Midasplayer. It was his game, and he was able to develop it in any way he pleased.

Persson may not have been happy with his job at Midasplayer. But he liked many of the people who worked there. One of them was Elin Zetterstrand, the company's online community coordinator. Zetterstrand shared Persson's love of video games. The two struck up a friendship. They played games together and eventually began dating.

Persson's contract with Midasplayer said that he wasn't allowed to develop his own games while he worked for the company. But at first, Midasplayer didn't enforce this rule. They let Persson continue with *Wurm Online* and other projects, free of interference. That changed in 2008, when Persson created a game called *Blast Passage*. Some of the games Persson had played in his youth inspired him to create this retro game. He was proud of the result. He sent an email to other workers at Midasplayer, inviting them to check out his creation.

The email caught the attention of the company's director, Lars Markgren. Markgren thought that *Blast*

In *Blast Passage,* players used the space bar and arrow keys to give commands, as they would have done in early 1980s computer games.

Passage was too similar to one of Midasplayer's games. He told Persson that he couldn't release it on his own. The exchange left Persson feeling sour. He dreamed of leaving Midasplayer to start his own gaming company. But he knew that the odds would be stacked against him, and he couldn't afford to go long without a paycheck. He felt trapped.

Persson wasn't ready to strike out on his own. However, he felt that it was time to start looking for a new job. It didn't take him long to find one. He accepted a position at Avalanche, one of Sweden's leading game developers. Avalanche developed games that were much bigger and more ambitious than Midasplayer. But Persson was still unhappy. To him, working at Avalanche felt like working in a factory. He was helping to assemble games, not creating them.

Persson didn't last long at Avalanche. He returned briefly to his old job at Midasplayer. But his attempts to work in the gaming industry seemed to be failing. He just wanted to escape. So, in early 2009, he took a job with a company called Jalbum. It wasn't even in the gaming industry. Jalbum made software for building online photo albums. But working there provided one benefit that he couldn't get at a gaming company. Jalbum had no interest in the games Persson made on his own time. Finally, he could have the best of both worlds. He would be bringing home a steady paycheck, and the games he created outside of his workplace would be his alone.

Programming Competitions

Persson is an active participant in programming competitions. One of the most popular is Ludum Dare, which is Latin for "to give a game." In this contest, programmers have just a few days or less to create a game that fits a certain theme.

In December 2011, Persson made a game for Ludum Dare called *Minicraft*. The adventure game was similar to the classic Nintendo title *The Legend of Zelda* with elements of *Minecraft*.

Sequels and new editions of *The Legend of Zelda* continue to be popular among gamers.

INTO THE CAVE

Persson worked for Jalbum during the day. At night and on the weekends, he threw himself into a new project. Persson thought back to his youth spent building with Lego and playing computer games. He imagined a game that would combine both of those passions. Players could use simple blocks to craft an entire world. It would be completely open, with players allowed to progress in any way they saw fit. This type of program, without levels or tasks to be completed in a certain order, is known as a sandbox game. At first, he named it *Cave Game*. In May 2009, he renamed it *Minecraft*. The name combined two elements of the game, mining for materials and crafting objects with them. It was also a tribute to *Warcraft*, a popular online game at the time.

Developing the game consumed Persson's time. Determined to finish it, he turned to online programming forums for advice. Finally, he had a working version of the game. He released it on May 17, 2009.

The game was still rough around the edges. It fell into a broad category known as indie (short for independent) games, a classification for games released by individuals or small organizations rather than big gaming companies. Persson had mostly worked alone, using the code from an existing game, *Infiniminer*, as the backbone for his creation. Yet even in its unfinished state, *Minecraft* caught the attention of gamers. It was both simple to learn and complicated to master. That

Minecraft players use computerized blocks to build all kinds of structures, such as this castle and forest.

meant that it appealed to casual newcomers as well as gaming veterans—a rare combination.

As the game's online community grew, working on the game and communicating with gamers took up more and more of Persson's time. But he also realized that he had tapped into something. *Minecraft* was different from anything else on the market, and gamers were responding.

Zetterstrand was at his side throughout and was among the first to play the game. She helped him test new features and gave him feedback when he made updates. Persson also invited feedback from the gaming community. He welcomed comments and suggestions. And soon he began charging for the game through a

This man plays *Warcraft: Reign of Chaos* in 2002. *Minecraft*'s name is a tribute to the popular *Warcraft* franchise.

website he'd made, Minecraft.net. It was a bold move. Many indie game developers make their money by advertising rather than sales. But Persson decided early on that he preferred to charge for the game itself. He also knew that if he was ever going to make a living from *Minecraft*, he'd need the steady income. Persson also offered a free version, but it lacked many of the features of the more finished product.

"The reason that I released the game so early was that I would never have been able to finish it otherwise," he later said. "Charging money was the same thing. I knew that I would never feel that it was good enough to put a price tag on. So I charged from the start."

RAPID GROWTH

The early versions of *Minecraft* were simple compared with what the game would become. Yet there was something about building structures with virtual blocks that caught fire. People took screenshots and videos of their creations and posted them online. It was the kind of word-of-mouth advertising that game developers dream of having.

At first, Persson tracked every sale with great interest. Every time someone paid for his game, he got an email. At first, that meant just a few emails every day. But as time

The creeper, the green rectangle monster on the right, was the first mob, or moving creature, in *Minecraft*. It was added in 2009.

Minecraft players use the crafting table to make things. This tool was originally called a workbench.

went on, his inbox swelled. As sales grew, he spent more time adding to the game, creating animals and monsters to inhabit the world his players built. He quit his job at Jalbum to work full time on *Minecraft*.

By June 2010, with the game about a year old, his inbox was collecting around four hundred sales notifications per day. It was no longer generating just enough income for Persson to scrape by. He was earning thousands of dollars every day—more money than he'd ever dreamed *Minecraft* could bring him.

The game continued to evolve. Persson created a version of the game that had cycles of day and night. During the day, players built their creations. At night, monsters roamed the land and players took shelter in what they had built. As Persson added more layers and options to the game, it just kept growing in popularity.

In August 2010, Persson met with executives from Valve, one of the biggest gaming developers in the world. Valve offered Persson a job. At one time, it would have been his dream job. But Persson turned it down.

Steve (*left*) has been part of *Minecraft* since its beginnings. Since 2015 players have had the option of playing as Alex, a female character, instead. Modern players can change either character's skin color too.

"Somehow, I felt that *Minecraft* was maybe my chance to create a Valve, rather than work at Valve," he said.

Persson realized that he needed to do more than just work on the game. He needed to build a company around it. So he, along with his friend and fellow programmer Jakob Porsér, started Mojang in Stockholm.

In November 2010, IGN.com, one of the leading websites in the gaming industry, gave *Minecraft* a glowing review. "As simple as this concept may seem, the reason so much buzz surrounds this title is the

Jakob Porsér (*left*) and Persson at a Swedish hockey game in 2015

Mojang employees work at their headquarters in Stockholm in 2013. The office includes board games, Lego, and a pool table.

sheer limitless potential it holds," wrote reviewer Jeremy Ashdown. "While you can make a shelter that consists of a hole in the ground, users have gone slightly mad creating massive superstructures and recreating well-known landmarks. . . . If *Minecraft* proves anything, it's that the age of the bedroom programmer is not over. This is a game developed by one guy that's gone on to be one of the best selling indie titles of all time; largely through word of mouth."

BUILDING THE BRAND

Persson understood that Mojang needed more than just one game. He and Porsér had long talked about another idea that blended elements of collectable card games and board games. They started to work on Mojang's next creation, titled *Scrolls*. Persson was involved in the game's development but in more of a supporting role. *Scrolls* was mainly Porsér's creation. Announced in 2011, it wasn't formally released until 2013. *Scrolls* was well received by critics. But it never made the kind of splash that *Minecraft* had. Mojang stopped development just two years after its release.

Mojang was busy designing new games. But *Minecraft* was still the company's centerpiece. As sales soared, the gaming industry showered Persson and *Minecraft* with awards. In March 2011, Persson and others from Mojang attended the Game Developers Conference (GDC) in San Francisco, California. There they collected four prizes in two awards ceremonies, including categories for best innovation, best debut, and audience favorite. "I'm so happy now you wouldn't believe it," Persson told his fans through his Twitter account.

Social media was Persson's main way of communicating with his growing number of fans. An entire community had built up around the game, with message boards, social media hubs, and fan conventions. As *Minecraft* grew larger and larger, he became a video game celebrity.

Persson's professional life was more successful than

As *Minecraft* grew in popularity, the game and its creator won multiple awards.

he could ever have dreamed. It was time for a big step in his personal life as well. In August of 2011, he and Zetterstrand married. Persson wore his trademark hat, a black fedora, for the ceremony. Mojang celebrated the wedding with a special "wedding weekend" promotion.

Persson shows off an award he received from the 2012 British Academy Games Awards.

Everyone who bought a copy of *Minecraft* over the weekend got a second copy for free to give to a loved one.

The official, finished version of *Minecraft* finally was released at MineCon in Las Vegas on November 18, 2011. The game's success had given its creator fame and fortune. But he was also feeling trapped by it and by the expectations of his fans. He grew more and more frustrated with managing the game, and he felt that his role in creating the game had ended.

A few weeks after MineCon, he made the announcement that shocked many of his fans. He was stepping away from the game he had created. He would turn over control of the game to Jens Bergensten, who had been helping Persson develop the game for more than a year. "[It's a] scary move, but I feel strangely confident," Persson said of the change. "I guess we've worked close enough for long enough for me to feel confident about it."

Persson on Piracy

One of the biggest problems game developers face is piracy. Many popular games are illegally copied, or pirated, by gamers who can't or won't pay for them. Many game developers go to great lengths to battle piracy, which most regard as theft.

Persson isn't one of them. In fact, he has embraced it. Once a gamer sent him a tweet, asking for a free download. The gamer said he thought he'd ask before downloading an illegal pirated copy of *Minecraft*.

Persson's response may have been a shock. "Just pirate it," he replied. "If you still like it when you can afford it in the future, buy it then. Also don't forget to feel bad. ;]"

He expanded on his views at the 2011 GDC. "Piracy is not theft," he said. "If you steal a car, the original is lost. If you copy a game, there are simply more of them in the world. There is no such thing as a 'lost sale.'"

Persson signs autographs for fans in Paris in 2012.

STRUGGLING WITH SUCCESS

Even while *Minecraft* continued to soar in popularity, Persson's life seemed to be spiraling out of control. In 2011 his father died of a self-inflicted gunshot wound. Persson had recently reconnected with his dad, and his death hit Persson hard. He and Zetterstrand had a daughter, Minna Almina Zelda Zetterstrand, but their marriage fell apart in 2012.

Persson fell into a depression. He didn't know how to deal with his newfound fame, and he struggled socially.

Persson began to obsess over the comments of internet trolls—people who post hateful messages on internet chat rooms or message boards. The success of *Minecraft* was so far beyond what he'd ever imagined that he found it difficult to find purpose in his life.

One of the problems plaguing Persson was the lack of challenge in his life. He wanted to do something new—something different. So, in 2012, he started work on a new game—one completely different from *Minecraft*. He came up with the idea for a space adventure game. He called it *0x10c*, pronounced "ten to the c."

Kids dressed as *Minecraft* characters attend the Fan Expo Vancouver convention in 2015.

The game failed before it ever launched. Persson suffered from the programmer's version of writer's block. He kept trying to develop the game, but by 2013, he realized it was hopeless. He abandoned the project, saying that the game simply wasn't any fun to play. Once again, the game developer was stuck in a rut.

CASHING IN

Persson had never been wealthy growing up. During his years at Midasplayer, he earned enough to get by, but he was far from rich. As *Minecraft* exploded in popularity, he was raking in millions of dollars. At first, he was cautious with his fortune. But that didn't last long.

Jens Bergensten (*left*) took over the development of *Minecraft* in 2011.

Social Media: The Good and the Bad

Social media, including websites such as Facebook and Twitter, has always been a big part of Persson's life. One could argue that *Minecraft* would never have been big without it. As an indie developer, Persson didn't use traditional advertising for his work. Instead, he relied on word of mouth. As people discovered the game, they posted about it on social media, spreading the word and bringing in new players.

Persson and his colleagues at Mojang understood the importance of social media. As the company grew, they used it to communicate with their players and build networks of gamers. For many, this sense of community was a big part of *Minecraft*'s appeal.

However, Persson has also seen some of the drawbacks of social media. Some of his posts have drawn criticism. In 2017, for instance, he posted tweets that some felt were insensitive to women and minorities. He quickly apologized for some of the tweets, but not everyone felt his apologies were sincere.

Persson developed a taste for luxury. He shopped for watches that cost more than $100,000. He took long, expensive vacations. He spent hundreds of thousands of dollars on parties. Meanwhile, many of his relationships suffered. His former wife was gone. His once friendly

Mojang coders at work in their Stockholm office in 2013.

relationship with Bergensten, who had helped launch *Minecraft*, turned cold.

When Mojang changed its terms of service, limiting the ways that players could make money in the game by selling resources to fellow players, Persson faced ridicule from many. Frustrated, he tweeted that he just wanted to sell his shares of Mojang and be done with it all.

By 2014 Persson was ready for change—big change. Microsoft, a giant in the computer industry, approached Persson about buying Mojang. Microsoft officials had seen Persson's tweet about wanting to sell his shares in the company. They wanted to find out if he was serious.

"I thought about it for a while and said, yeah I would actually really like to be not responsible for this for a while," Persson later said. "I didn't want to do a big complicated thing where I'd get partial ownership for a while and I'd still feel like I'm still responsible for someone else's input. I just wanted a clean break."

It was a big change in thinking for Persson. The idea of selling off his company to a tech giant like Microsoft probably would have horrified him when he'd first created Mojang. But his views had changed. And the offer on the

Minecraft fan merchandise includes stuffed animals, Lego sets, and more.

table was huge. In September 2014, the two sides came to an agreement. Microsoft would buy Mojang. The price tag was staggering: $2.5 billion. Persson was already incredibly wealthy. Suddenly, he was a billionaire. While many of Mojang's employees would remain on staff after the deal, Persson would not be one of them. He was leaving his company behind for good.

News of the deal was a shock to many *Minecraft* players. Many worried what would happen once their beloved game was in the hands of a giant company like Microsoft. After the deal was announced, Persson tried to explain to his fans why he had agreed to it. "Thank you for turning *Minecraft* into what it has become, but there are too many of you, and I can't be responsible for something this big," he said. The game's fan base had become huge. In 2014 more than one hundred million people were registered *Minecraft* players.

About the sale, Persson said, "In one sense, it belongs to Microsoft now. In a much bigger sense, it's belonged to all of you for a long time, and that will never change." Persson later added that selling Mojang had not been about money. It had been about preserving his own mental health.

The sale became official on November 6, 2014. At the end of the workday, Persson packed his things and left his office. He wasn't sure what to do or how to say goodbye. His solution was simple. He didn't say goodbye. He merely walked out the door. A remarkable chapter in his life had ended.

Persson outbid stars Beyoncé and Jay-Z, among other potential buyers, for this mansion. The home is so large that it has fifteen bathrooms!

LIFE AFTER *MINECRAFT*

Persson was thirty-five when he walked away from Mojang. He wondered what to do with the rest of his life. His work had started with a passion for computers and video games. So that's where he turned. Only this time, he wasn't focused on making the games. He spent his time playing them instead. He also took a trip to Miami, Florida, with Porsér and some others who had a stake in Mojang. There, they celebrated the sale and their newfound fortunes.

Persson wasn't shy about spending his fortune. He bought a mansion in the Los Angeles, California, area for $70 million. Then he threw a huge party to show it off.

In 2016 Persson received a Pioneer Award from the Game Developers Choice Awards for his work on *Minecraft*.

Though he found enjoyment from his trips and parties, Persson still struggled with depression. He felt a lack of purpose in his life.

"The problem with getting everything is that you run out of reasons to keep trying, and human interaction becomes impossible," he wrote on Twitter. "Hanging out . . . with famous friends and partying with famous people, able to do whatever I want, and I've never felt more isolated."

Persson's comments drew sharp criticism. Some people mocked him, calling him the whining billionaire. They pointed out a personal vacation he'd recently taken, during which he'd spent hundreds of thousands of dollars partying in Las Vegas. Persson ended up posting an apology for his tweet.

Even though he called himself retired, programming was still in Persson's blood. He and Porsér started a new gaming company called Rubberbrain. But they didn't

Persson and his company, Rubberbrain, have homes in this area of Stockholm.

make any new games for the company. "It's like a daycare for us," he explained, "grown-up daycare. It's good to have some place to go."

What does the future hold for Persson and Rubberbrain? No one is sure. When he created *Minecraft*, Persson made himself one of the biggest stars of the gaming world. Will he follow it up with something new? Or will he fade out of the public eye as a self-made billionaire? His fans can't wait to find out what will be next.

IMPORTANT DATES

1979 Markus Alexej Persson is born on June 1 in Stockholm, Sweden.

1987 At eight years old, he programs his first game, a text-based adventure.

1997 Persson takes his first computer programming job.

2002 He takes a job at Game Federation, a video game distributor.

2003 He releases a beta version of his massively multiplayer online game, *Wurm Online*.

2004 He takes a job as a game programmer for Midasplayer.

2009 He creates *Minecraft*. He releases the alpha version on May 17.

2010 *Minecraft* grows in popularity. Persson founds a new company, Mojang.

2011 Persson marries Elin Zetterstrand in August. *Minecraft 1.0* is officially released at MineCon in Las Vegas, Nevada, in November.

2012 Persson begins work on a space adventure titled *0x10c*, but the game is never officially released.

Persson's daughter, Minna, is born in April.

2013 Mojang announces that versions of *Minecraft* are forthcoming for video game consoles including PlayStation 4 and Xbox One.

2014 Microsoft buys Mojang for $2.5 billion. Persson leaves the company he built.

Persson buys a Los Angeles, California, mansion for $70 million.

2017 Persson stirs up controversy on Twitter for posts that some considered insensitive to minorities and women. He later apologizes for the posts.

SOURCE NOTES

7–8 Daniel Goldberg and Linus Larsson, Minecraft, *Second Edition: The Unlikely Tale of Markus "Notch" Persson and the Game That Changed Everything* (New York: Seven Stories, 2015), 13.

8 Ibid.

11 Alex Handy, "Interview: Markus 'Notch' Persson Talks Making *Minecraft*," *Gamasutra*, March 23, 2010, https://www.gamasutra.com/view/news/27719/Interview_Markus_Notch_Persson_Talks_Making_Minecraft.php.

13 Malin Roos, "The Story of Markus 'Notch' Persson," *Expressen*, January 4, 2015, https://www.expressen.se/nyheter/the-story-of-markus-notch-persson/.

22 Goldberg and Larsson, *Unlikely Tale*, 99.

26 Ibid. 127.

26–27 Jeremy Ashdown, "This Is *Minecraft*," *IGN.com*, November 11, 2010, http://www.ign.com/articles/2010/11/11/this-is-minecraft.

28 Goldberg and Larsson, *Unlikely Tale*, 166.

31 Mike Nelson, "Notch Hands *Minecraft* Reigns to Jeb," *GameSpy*, December 2, 2011, http://pc.gamespy.com/pc/minecraft/1213830p1.html.

31 Dave Thier, "*Minecraft* Creator Notch Tells Players to Pirate His Game," *Forbes*, January 12, 2012, https://www.forbes.com/sites/davidthier/2012/01/12/minecraft-creator-notch-tells-players-to-pirate-his-game/#201b951d4eb6.

31 Ibid.

33 Jeffrey Matulef, "Notch Shows Off First Footage of *0x10^C*," *Eurogamer*, April 10, 2012, http://www.eurogamer.net/articles/2012-10-04-notch-shows-off-first-footage-of-0x10c.

37 Ryan Mac, "*Minecraft*'s Markus Persson Tells All on His Sale to Microsoft, His $70 Million Home and What's Next," *Forbes*, March 3, 2015, https://www.forbes.com/sites/ryanmac/2015/03/03/minecraft-markus-persson-notch-interview-microsoft-sale/#26add46fdb04.

38 Brett Molina, "Microsoft to Acquire 'Minecraft' Maker Mojang for $2.5B," *USA Today*, September 15, 2014, https://www.usatoday.com/story/tech/gaming/2014/09/15/microsoft-minecraft/15658383/.

38 Ibid.

40 Tom Leonard, "The Whining Billionaire Who Says Being Rich Is Sheer Hell: Inside the Life That Minecraft Founder Markus Persson Says Has Been Ruined by Too Much Money," *Daily Mail.com*, September 2, 2015, http://www.dailymail.co.uk/news/article-3220333/The-whining-billionaire-says-rich-sheer-hell-Inside-life-Minecraft-founder-Markus-Persson-says-ruined-money.html.

41 Mac, "Persson Tells All."

SELECTED BIBLIOGRAPHY

Ashdown, Jeremy. "This Is *Minecraft*." *IGN.com*, November 11, 2010. http://www.ign.com/articles/2010/11/11/this-is-minecraft.

Cheshire, Tom. "Changing the Game: How Notch Made *Minecraft* a Cult Hit." *Wired*, September 15, 2014. http://www.wired.co.uk/article/changing-the-game.

Goldberg, Daniel, and Linus Larsson. Minecraft, *Second Edition: The Unlikely Tale of Markus "Notch" Persson and the Game That Changed Everything*. New York: Seven Stories, 2015.

Handy, Alex. "Interview: Markus 'Notch' Persson Talks Making *Minecraft*." *Gamasutra*, March 23, 2010. https://www.gamasutra.com/view/news/27719/Interview_Markus_Notch_Persson_Talks_Making_Minecraft.php.

Mac, Ryan. "*Minecraft*'s Markus Persson Tells All on His Sale to Microsoft, His $70 Million Home and What's Next." *Forbes*, March 3, 2015. https://www.forbes.com/sites/ryanmac/2015/03/03/minecraft-markus-persson-notch-interview-microsoft-sale/#26add46fdb04.

McDougall, Jaz. "Community Heroes: Notch, for *Minecraft*." *PC Gamer*, July 29, 2010. http://www.pcgamer.com/community-heroes-notch-for-minecraft/.

Parkin, Simon. "The Creator." *New Yorker*, April 5, 2013. https://www.newyorker.com/tech/elements/the-creator.

Peisner, David. "The Wizard of *Minecraft*." *Rolling Stone*, May 7, 2014. https://www.rollingstone.com/culture/news/the-wizard-of-minecraft-20140507.

Roos, Malin. "The Story of Markus 'Notch' Persson." *Expressen*, January 4, 2015. https://www.expressen.se/nyheter/the-story-of-markus-notch-persson/.

FURTHER READING

BOOKS

Cornell, Kari. Minecraft *Creator Markus "Notch" Persson.* Minneapolis: Lerner Publications, 2016. Learn more about Persson, who started creating his own computer games at the age of eight.

Keppeler, Jill. *The Inventors of* Minecraft*: Markus "Notch" Persson and His Coding Team.* New York: PowerKids, 2018. Check out this biography of the team that built the famous video game.

Martin, Chris. Minecraft: *The Business behind the Makers of* Minecraft. Minneapolis: Lerner Publications, 2016. Learn about the development of the global phenomenon of *Minecraft.*

Woodcock, Jon. *Coding Games in Scratch.* New York: DK, 2016. Try your hand at using code to make your own games.

WEBSITES

How Do Computers Work?
http://www.explainthatstuff.com/howcomputerswork.html
Check out an overview of computer history at this site.

How Making a Video Game Works
https://electronics.howstuffworks.com/making-a-video-game.htm
Learn the basics of video games, from how they're built to how this career field is changing and growing.

Minecraft: Official Site
https://minecraft.net/en-us/
This site can answer any questions you have about *Minecraft*, from those who know it best.

Minecraft Wiki: Beginner's Guide
https://minecraft.gamepedia.com/Tutorials/Beginner%27s_guide
If you've never played the game invented by Persson, this site will guide you through how to start.

INDEX